THE
TALL BOOK
OF
BIBLE
STORIES

RETOLD BY
KATHARINE GIBSON
ILLUSTRATED BY
TED CHAIKO

HARPER & ROW, PUBLISHERS   EST. 1817

CONTENTS

THE OLD TESTAMENT

THE NEW TESTAMENT

THE OLD TESTAMENT

THE CREATION

In the beginning God created the heaven and
the earth. And the earth was without form or
shape. Darkness was upon the face of the
waters. And the Spirit of God moved upon
the face of the waters.

And God said, "Let there be light."

And there was light. And God saw the light,
that it was good. And God divided the light
from the darkness. And God called the light
Day, and the darkness He called Night. This
was the first day.

10

And God said, "Let there be a sky in the midst of the waters and let it divide the water from the water."

And God called the sky Heaven. And God saw that it was good. This was the second day.

And God said, "Let the waters under the heaven be gathered together in one place, and let dry land appear."

And it was so; and God called the dry land Earth, and the waters He called the Seas.

And God said, "Let the earth bring forth grass, and the seeds of the field. Let the fruit tree bring forth fruit upon the earth."

This was the third day.

And God said, "Let there be light in the heavens to divide the day from the night, and let them be the signs for the seasons, the days, and the years."

And God made two great lights: the greater to rule by day, the lesser by night. He made the stars, also. And God saw that it was good. This was the fourth day.

And God made great whales and every living thing that moves through the waters, and every winged bird that flies above the earth. And God blessed them. And this was the fifth day.

And God said; "Let the earth bring forth living creatures, cattle and creeping things, and beasts of every kind."

And God created man in His own image.
And God said to the man, "Behold, I have
given you power over the fish of the sea and
the birds of the air and over everything that
creeps upon the earth, and over the beasts and
the cattle of the field." And God said, "Behold,
I have given you every herb-bearing seed
which is upon the face of the earth, and every
tree; to you it shall be for food."

And it was so. And God saw everything
He had made; and behold, it was good. This
was the sixth day.

Thus the heavens and the earth were finished. And on the seventh day God ended His
work which He had done. And He rested on
the seventh day. Then God blessed the seventh
day and called it holy, because in it He had
rested from all His work.

THE GARDEN
OF EDEN

And in the day that the Lord God made the earth and the heavens, He planted a garden eastward in Eden. In the light He planted it, and in the garden grew every tree that is pleasant to the sight and good for food. The tree of life was in the midst of the garden. And also in the garden was the tree of the knowledge of good and evil. Wide were its branches, and its fruit was round and smooth.

The Lord God created man in His image; out of the dust of the earth He created him. He put man in the garden to care for it and keep it. And the Lord God commanded the man, saying:

"Of every tree of the garden you may eat, but of the tree of the knowledge of good and evil you shall not eat, for on the day you eat of it you shall surely die."

And the Lord God said, "It is not good that the man should be alone; I will make a helpmate for him."

And out of the ground the Lord God formed every beast of the field and every fowl of the air. Dust became the song of the bird, the strength of the lion, the gentleness of the lamb, the fleetness of the deer, and the stealth of the red fox.

The Lord God brought all living creatures unto the man whose name was Adam to see what he would call them; and whatsoever Adam called every one, that was its name forever after. But Adam was alone; there was not found a helpmate for him.

And the Lord God caused a deep sleep to fall upon Adam, and he slept; and the Lord took one of his ribs, and closed up the flesh so there was no mark upon it. From the rib which the Lord God had taken from man, He made a woman, and brought her unto the man. And Adam said:

> *This is now bone of my bones,*
> *And flesh of my flesh;*
> *She shall be called Woman,*
> *Because she was taken out of Man.*

Therefore shall a man leave his father and his mother, and shall cleave to his wife, and they two shall dwell together.

From that day on, Adam and the woman lived in peace in the Garden of Eden. They did not have to hunt for food or till the soil. They were young and beautiful as the morning. They knew neither good nor evil. For like the stars and the fresh-flowing waters, they were but newly made.

Now, of all the animals that the Lord had made, the wisest and most crafty was the serpent. In that time, he walked like other beasts; and his voice was sweeter than honey and gentler than the doves. He spoke to the woman:

"Has the Lord God said, 'You shall not eat of every tree of the garden'?"

And the woman answered, "We may eat of the fruit of the trees in the garden, but not the fruit of the tree of the knowledge of good and evil. For God has said, 'You shall not eat of it, neither shall you touch it, or you shall die.' "

The serpent said unto the woman, "You shall not surely die, for God knows that in the day you taste of the fruit, then shall your eyes be opened and you shall be as gods, knowing good from evil."

The woman saw that the tree was good for food, and that it was pleasant to the eyes and a tree to be desired. For it would make her and Adam wise.

She took the fruit and ate of it.

She called Adam her husband to her, and gave also to him, and he ate. And the eyes of the two were opened, and they now had knowledge of good and evil.

Now they heard the voice of the Lord God, walking in the garden in the cool of the day. Adam and his wife hid themselves from the presence of the Lord God amongst the trees of the garden.

And the Lord God called to Adam and said unto him: "Man, come forth."

And Adam said: "I heard Your voice in the garden, and I was afraid, because I was naked."

And the Lord God said: "Who told you that you were naked? Did you eat of the tree which I commanded that you should not eat?"

And the man said: "The woman whom You gave to be with me, she gave me of the tree, and I did eat."

And the Lord God said unto the woman: "What is this you have done?"

And the woman answered: "The serpent tempted me, and I ate. His voice was sweeter than honey and more gentle than the doves."

19

The Lord God said unto the serpent:

Because thou hast done this,
Cursed art thou above all cattle,
And above every beast of the field;
Upon thy belly shalt thou go,
And dust shalt thou eat,
All the days of thy life.
And I will put enmity between
    thee and the woman
And between her young and thine.
He shall bruise thy head,
And thou shalt bruise his heel.

Unto the woman He said:

I will greatly multiply thy pain;
In pain thou shalt bring forth children;
And your husband shall rule over thee.

And unto Adam He said:

Because thou hearkened unto the voice
    of thy wife,
And have eaten of the fruit of which
    I commanded of thee,
Saying, "Thou shalt not eat of it,"
Cursed is the ground for thy sake,
In sorrow shalt thou eat of it
    all the days of thy life.
Thorns also and thistles shall
    it bring forth to thee,
And thou shalt eat the herb of the field;
In the sweat of thy face shalt thou
    eat bread
Till thou return unto the ground,
For out of it wast thou taken.
For dust thou art,
And unto dust shalt thou return.

Now Adam named his wife Eve, which means first woman and mother of all the children of the earth.

And the Lord God said, "Behold, the man is become as one of Us, to know good and evil. And now, lest he put forth his hand and take also of the tree of life and eat and live forever, I will send him and the woman forth from the Garden of Eden."

And God drove them out, both the man and the woman. And Adam and Eve, sorrowing, went out together.

From that day forth, Adam toiled in the fields for all the bread that he and Eve did eat, they and their children. And Eve worked to spin and weave cloth that they might be clothed. And because they had eaten the fruit of which the Lord had commanded, "You shall not eat," never did Adam and Eve or any of the children of men return again to the garden. For at the east of the Garden of Eden the Lord God placed angels, and a flaming sword which turned every way to guard the tree of life.

NOAH'S ARK

Now as the days and years passed, the children of Adam and Eve and their children's children were many. They grew to be a great people; and they filled the earth. Because Eve ate the fruit of the tree which the Lord told her not to eat, and gave of the fruit to her husband Adam, all the children of men knew what things were good, and what things evil. But none in all the world did the things that were good, save one. His name was Noah.

And the Lord spoke to Noah:

"I will bring a flood of waters upon the earth; it will cover the valleys and the hills, even the mountains it will cover. Everything that is on earth will die, for the children of men have done those things which are evil. But build a boat, an ark out of gopher wood. You shall cover it with pitch inside and out. A window shall you put in the ark; the door shall you set in the side. With three stories shall you build it.

"I will make a covenant with you. You shall go into the ark, you and your wife, and your sons and their wives. And of every living thing, all. the beasts of the field and birds of the air, you shall take two of every kind. They shall go into the ark. So shall they be alive with you.

"And you shall take food that is good for man, and food that is good for the beasts of the field, and food that is good for the birds of the air. And you shall gather it, and bring it into the ark that you may eat and not be hungry, and that the beasts and the birds shall not want."

Noah and his three sons, who were Shem, Ham, and Japheth, built the ark even as the Lord said. And Noah went into the ark, and his wife and his sons' wives. And the beasts of the field and the birds of the air went into the ark, two by two.

And after seven days had passed, the flood of waters was upon the earth. The fountains of the great deep opened up and the windows of heaven were opened. And the rain fell for forty days and forty nights. The waters lifted the ark from the earth. It floated upon the water. The waters covered the valleys and the hills, even the mountains, were covered.

In all the world only Noah lived, and his wife and his three sons and their wives. In all the world only those beasts of the field and birds of the air lived that went into the ark two by two.

And the waters covered the earth for a hundred and fifty days. And the ark floated on the waters above the valleys and the hills, even above the mountains it floated.

And God remembered Noah and every living thing in the ark. He sent a wind over the earth. The fountains of the deep and the windows of heaven were stopped; the rains no longer fell. The waters grew less, and in the tenth month the tops of the mountains could be seen.

And it came to pass that Noah opened up the window of the ark which he had made. And he sent a dove out of the ark to see if the waters were gone off the face of the earth. But the dove found no rest for the sole of her foot; she came again to the ark, for the waters covered the earth. Then Noah put out his hand and took her again into the ark.

And Noah waited yet another seven days and sent the dove forth again. And the dove came to him in the evening, and in her mouth was an olive leaf she had plucked. So Noah knew the waters had gone from the earth.

The Lord spoke to Noah, "Go forth out of the ark, you and your wife and your three sons, Shem, Ham, and Japheth, and their wives with them. And all the beasts in the ark, let them come out; and all the birds of the air, let them come out."

And Noah lifted the cover of the ark and opened wide the door, and he and his wife and his sons and their wives came once again to the earth. And out of the ark, two by two, came all the beasts, and all the birds of the air.

And Noah built an altar and prayed to the Lord a prayer of thanksgiving.

And the Lord said:

"I will not again send the waters upon the earth, neither will I hurt any living thing. Forever shall there be seedtime and harvest, and cold and heat, and summer and winter, and day and night. So shall it be.

"And I shall make a covenant with you and with your wife, with your three sons and with your sons' wives. And I shall make a covenant with every beast of the field and every bird of the air that was in the ark. This is the sign. I will set a rainbow in the cloud. It shall be the sign of a promise between you and Me. And when I bring the clouds, I will also bring the rainbow And I will remember the promise between God and every creature of the earth."

And Noah and his wife, and his three sons and their wives, lived upon the earth. They cared for the fields, and the beasts of the field and the birds of the air. When the rain fell, and the clouds came, the Lord sent the rainbow. It was the sign of his promise to all living creatures. And there was no great flood of waters from that day forth.

THE STORY OF ABRAHAM AND ISAAC

Now one of the descendants of Noah was Abraham. Sarah, the wife of Abraham, bore him a son in his old age. And Sarah said, rejoicing, "God has made me to laugh so that all that hear me will laugh, for I have borne a son, Isaac, in my old age."

And it came to pass, when Isaac was well grown, that the Lord came unto Abraham and said, "Abraham, behold, here I am."

And He said, "Take now your only son, Isaac, whom you love, and get you into the land of Moriah. Slay Isaac and offer him there for a burnt offering upon one of the mountains which I will tell you of."

And Abraham rose up early in the morning and saddled his ass, and took two of his young men with him, and Isaac his son, and cut the wood for the burnt offering and went toward the place of which God had told him. Then on the third day, Abraham lifted up his eyes and saw the place afar off. And Abraham said unto the young men, "Abide ye here with the ass; and I and the lad will go yonder and worship and come again to you."

Abraham took the wood for the burnt offering, and laid it upon Isaac, his son. And Abraham took the fire in his hand, and a knife, and they went both of them together.

And Isaac spoke unto Abraham, his father, and said, "My father."

And Abraham answered, "Here am I, my son."

Isaac said, "My father, behold the fire and the wood, but where is the lamb for the burnt offering?"

And Abraham spoke, saying, "My son, God will provide Himself a lamb for the burnt offering." And they both went on together.

They came to the place of which God had told Abraham. And Abraham built an altar there and laid the wood in order, and bound Isaac his son. And Abraham stretched forth his hand, and he took the knife to slay his son for an offering even as the Lord had commanded.

And the angel of the Lord called unto him out of heaven and said, "Abraham, Abraham."

And Abraham answered, "Here am I."

And the angel said, "Lay not your hand upon the lad, neither do you anything unto him. For now I know you fear God, seeing you have not withheld your son, your only son, from me."

And Abraham lifted up his eyes and beheld a ram caught in a thicket by his horns. And Abraham went and took the ram and offered him up for a burnt offering instead of his son. And Abraham called the place Jehovah-jireh: as it is said to this day, "In the mount of the Lord it shall be seen."

JOSEPH AND
HIS BROTHERS

And it came to pass that when it was time for Isaac's son Jacob to marry, he went into the land of his father's people and took as his wife Rachel, the daughter of Laban. And Rachel bore him a son, who was called Joseph.

Joseph, being seventeen years old, tended his father's flocks with his brothers. But Jacob loved Joseph more than all his other children, and he made Joseph a coat of many colors. When the brothers saw that their father loved Joseph most, they hated Joseph.

Now Joseph dreamed a dream, and he told his brothers. He said unto them:

"Hear, I pray you, this dream which I have dreamed. For behold, we were binding sheaves of wheat in the field; and lo, my sheaf arose and stood upright, and your sheaves stood round about and bowed low before my sheaf."

His brothers said to him, "Shall you indeed reign over us, and shall you be ruler over us?" And they hated him yet more for his words.

Then Joseph dreamed yet another dream, and told his brothers: "Behold, the sun and the moon and eleven stars bowed before me."

And Joseph told the dream to his father also, and his father rebuked him, and said unto him, "What is this dream that you have dreamed? Shall I and your mother and your eleven brothers come to bow ourselves to earth before you?"

And Joseph's brothers were angry with the lad; but his father remembered the dream.

Now Joseph's brothers went to a distant place to feed their father's flocks. And Jacob said to Joseph, "I will send you unto your brothers. See whether it be well with them and with the flocks, and bring me word."

So Joseph went out from his father's house, and came near unto his brothers. And when they saw him afar off, they said one to another:

"Behold, this dreamer comes. Now, therefore, let us slay him and cast him into a pit, and we will say, 'An evil beast has devoured him, and we shall see what will become of his dreams."

And Joseph's brother Reuben heard it, and said, "Let us not kill him. Shed no blood, but cast him into this pit that is in the wilderness, and lay no hand upon him."

Reuben spoke thus so that he might take Joseph and bring him in safety to his father.

But when Reuben went away to tend his flock, the other brothers stripped Joseph of his coat of many colors, and they took him and cast him into an empty pit.

And they lifted up their eyes, and behold, a company of Ishmaelites came from the land of Gilead with their camels, bearing spices and balm and myrrh, carrying them down to Egypt. And one of the brothers, Judah, said:

"What gain is it if we leave our brother here to die? Come, let us sell him to the Ishmaelites, and let not our hand be upon him, for he is our brother and our flesh."

His brothers were content. They lifted Joseph out of the pit and sold him to the Ishmaelites for twenty pieces of silver. And the Ishmaelites brought Joseph into Egypt.

Now Reuben had been watching his flocks. When he came again to the pit and saw that Joseph was not there, he rent his clothes in wrath and terror. And he returned unto his brothers and said, "The child is gone; and I, whither shall I go?"

And his brothers took Joseph's coat and dipped it in the blood of a young goat they had killed. And they brought the coat of many colors to their father Jacob, and said, "This have we found. Say now whether or not this is your son's coat?"

Joseph's father knew it; and he said, "It is my son's coat; an evil beast has devoured him. He lives no more."

And Jacob rent his clothes, and wore sackcloth, and mourned for many days; nor would he be comforted.

And Jacob said, "I will go down into the grave mourning my son." Thus the father wept for his son Joseph.

Now when Joseph was brought down to Egypt, Potiphar, who was an officer of Pharaoh, King of Egypt, and captain of the guard, bought Joseph from the Ishmaelites. And the Lord was with Joseph, and Joseph found grace in the sight of his master Potiphar. And Potiphar made Joseph overseer in his house and over all he had.

Joseph was a goodly person and fair in the sight of men. But Potiphar's wife spoke evil words against Joseph, and he was cast into prison.

Even here the Lord was with Joseph and showed him mercy. For it came to pass that the butler of the King of Egypt had angered his master and he, also, was cast into prison. And the butler dreamed a dream, and Joseph said unto him, "Why do you look so sad?"

And the butler told his dream, saying:

"In my dream, behold, a vine was before me, and on the vine were three branches, and the vine budded; her blossoms shot forth; and the clusters brought forth ripe grapes. And Pharaoh's cup was in my hand, and I took the grapes and pressed them into Pharaoh's cup, and I gave the cup into Pharaoh's hand."

And Joseph said, "This is the meaning of it: Within three days shall Pharaoh send for you and restore you unto your place, and you shall again give Pharaoh his cup, and again you shall be his butler. But, I pray you, think of me when it is well with you. Speak of me unto Pharaoh. For, indeed, I have done nothing that they should put me into the dungeon."

It came to pass on the third day, which was Pharaoh's birthday, that Pharaoh made a feast unto all his servants. And he restored the chief butler to his place, and again the man gave to Pharaoh his cup. But in his happiness, he forgot Joseph, and the promise he had made in prison.

At the end of two full years, Pharaoh dreamed an evil dream. He called his butler to him and spoke:

"In my dream I beheld seven cows, fat and well-favored; they did feed in a meadow. And seven other cows came up after them, poor and lean. And the lean did eat up the seven fat cows; but when they had eaten, they were as ill-favored as in the beginning. And again I dreamed, and I saw seven ears of wheat come up on one stalk, full and good. And behold, seven ears that were withered, thin, and blasted sprang up after them. And the seven thin ears devoured and ate the seven good ears. Now, I told this dream unto the magicians, but none could tell me its meaning."

Then the chief butler related unto Pharaoh how Joseph had read his dream aright. And Pharaoh sent and called Joseph, and they brought him out of the dungeon.

When he had heard Pharoah's dream, he said: "The dreams of the Pharoah are one. The seven good cows are seven years, and the seven full ears of wheat are seven years; and the seven lean cows are seven years, and the seven blasted ears are seven years. What God is about to do, He shows unto Pharaoh. Behold, there shall come seven years of great plenty throughout all the land of Egypt; and there shall arise after them seven years of famine, and all the years of plenty shall be forgotten in the land of Egypt.

"Now, therefore, let the Pharoah find a man both strong and wise, and let the Pharaoh place this man over all the land of Egypt; and let this man and the officers under him take up the fifth part of the grain in the land of Egypt in the good years. And let the food be kept for the years of famine, that the people of Egypt perish not."

Pharaoh heard these things, and he said unto his men, "Can we find another such man as this?" And he said to Joseph, "You shall be over my house, and over the people. Only I shall be greater than you."

Thus Pharaoh made Joseph ruler over all the land of Egypt. And Joseph went through the land of Egypt, telling the people that grain must be stored against the years of famine.

Now it came to pass after seven years that the great famine came in all countries. But there was food in Egypt for the people.

When Jacob the father of Joseph heard there was grain in Egypt, he sent Joseph's brothers to buy of it. Joseph was governor in the land, and sold grain to all the people that came thither. But Joseph's brothers knew him not, and they bowed themselves low before him.

Joseph knew his brothers, but made himself strange unto them. He commanded that their sacks be filled with grain, and that they be given food for their journey. And so they returned to their father Jacob.

A second time Jacob sent his sons to the land of Egypt. Joseph welcomed them to his house and gave them to eat and drink. And they took from their sacks presents they had brought—a little balm, a little honey, spices, myrrh, nuts, and almonds. But yet they knew Joseph not.

And Joseph's heart yearned over them; and after much time had passed, he made himself known unto them. And he wept aloud, and said: "I am Joseph; does my father yet live?"

His brothers could not answer him, for they were troubled and filled with fear.

And Joseph said, "Come here to me, I pray you." And they came near.

And Joseph said, "God has made me lord of all Egypt. Haste you and go to my father and tell him of my glory in Egypt, and you shall bring my father unto me."

And they went on their way and came into the land of Canaan unto Jacob their father, and told him, saying, "Joseph is yet alive, and he is governor of all Egypt."

And Jacob's heart was faint, for he believed them not. And they told him the words of Joseph, and Jacob's spirit grew strong again. And he said, "It is enough. Joseph, my son, is yet alive. I will go and see him before I die."

And they took their cattle and their goods and went into Egypt, Jacob and his sons, his sons' sons with him; his daughters and his sons' daughters. And he sent one unto Joseph as a messenger. And Joseph made ready his chariot and went to meet Jacob his father.

And Jacob said unto Joseph, "Now let me die, since I have seen your face, because you are yet alive."

And Jacob and Joseph's brothers dwelt with Joseph; and great was their prospering. And Jacob called his sons to him, and said, "Gather you together, that I may tell you what will befall you in the days that are to come."

And of Joseph, he spoke:

> Joseph is a fruitful bough,
> Even a fruitful bough by a well,
> Whose branches run over the wall:
> The archers have sorely grieved him,
> And shot at him, and hated him:
> But his bow abode in strength,
> And the arms of his hands were made strong
> By the hands of the mighty God of Jacob . . .
> The blessings of the fathers have prevailed
> Above the blessings of many generations
> Unto the utmost bound of the everlasting hills;
> They shall be upon the head of Joseph,
> And on the crown of him that was separate
>   from his brethren.

Thus did Jacob bless Joseph and praise him; for Jacob loved Joseph more than all his other children.

MOSES IN
THE BULRUSHES

Now the children of Jacob, who was also called
Israel, and their children stayed in Egypt and
multiplied and became mighty. But after many
years, a new Pharaoh arose who remembered
not Joseph's good deeds.

He hardened his heart against the children
of Israel who dwelt in his lands. For he feared
their strength and their numbers. Therefore
Pharaoh set taskmasters over the Israelites to
punish and burden them. They were made to
build treasure cities, and to toil in the fields.
And their days were bitter. Yet they grew
ever stronger, and their numbers increased.

Then the Pharaoh sent forth a decree, saying,
"Every man-child born of the people of Israel
shall be slain, and every daughter saved alive."

Now there were in the land a man and a woman of the tribe of Joseph's brother Levi, who had a son born to them, a goodly child. And the mother in fear hid the child three months. And when she could no longer hide him, she made for him an ark of bulrushes, a cradle of reeds, and daubed it with pitch so that it would not sink. She put the child in it and laid it among the reeds and water lilies by the river bank. And the child's sister awaited far off to see what would be done.

Now the daughter of Pharaoh, proud and richly robed, came with her maidens to bathe in the river; and when she saw the ark among the reeds, she sent her maid to fetch it. When she opened it, she saw the child, and behold, the child wept. And she had pity on him, and said, "This is one of the Hebrew children."

Then the sister of the child drew near, and said to Pharaoh's daughter, "Shall I go and call to you a nurse from the Hebrew women, that she may care for the child?"

And Pharaoh's daughter said to her, "Go."

The child's sister went and called her mother. And Pharaoh's daughter said to her, "Take this child away and care for him, and I will bring you wages. And my word shall be a seal of safekeeping, both yours and the child's."

And the child's mother took him and cared for him.

Now the child grew, and when he had become a lad, the mother brought him again to Pharaoh's daughter. And Pharaoh's daughter said, "He shall be my son. And his name shall be called Moses, because I drew him out of the water."

And when Moses became a man he went among his brethren, the children of Israel, and looked on their burden. And the Lord appeared unto Moses out of the midst of a burning bush, saying:

"You shall lead My people out of the land of the Egyptian and bring them to a goodly land and large, a land flowing with milk and honey, even the land of Canaan."

And Moses said unto God, "Who am I, that I should go unto Pharaoh and that I should bring the children of Israel out of Egypt?"

And the Lord said, "Certainly I will be with you. And as a sign that I have chosen you, when you have brought the Hebrew people out of Egypt, you shall serve God upon the mountain."

And, as it was said that day, Moses was chosen by the Lord to lead the children of Israel out of the fields of bondage, free from the hand of Pharaoh.

CROSSING
THE RED SEA

And it came to pass that the Lord said unto Moses, "You shall speak unto Pharaoh, that he send the children of Israel out of his land."

Moses went to Pharaoh, and Pharaoh promised to let the Hebrews go free. But then Pharaoh hardened his heart again, and would not let the people go.

Now the Lord showed many signs and wonders in the land of Egypt. He turned the river of the Egyptians to blood and caused frogs to come upon the land. He changed the dust of the land, that it became lice; and sent a swarm of flies into the house of Pharaoh and into all the houses of Egypt. He brought death to the cattle, the oxen, the asses, and the sheep of the fields. But still Pharaoh would not let the people go as he had promised Moses.

Then the Lord sent upon the Egyptians a plague of boils, and on the land there was hail, thunder, and fire.

Locusts covered the face of the earth, and not a green thing remained in the trees or in the herbs of the field.

A thick darkness fell upon the Egyptians; and they saw not one another nor rose from their dwellings for three days.

Still was Pharaoh's heart hardened, and he would not let the children of Israel depart from the land of Egypt.

And the Lord said unto Moses, "Yet will I bring one plague more upon Pharaoh. Afterward will he let you go hence."

And the Lord smote all the firstborn in the land of Egypt so that they died, from the firstborn of Pharaoh who sat upon his throne, even unto the firstborn of the maidservant in the mill and all the firstborn beasts. But the Lord passed over the houses of the children of Israel and did not suffer one to be destroyed.

And the Lord said unto Moses, "And it shall come to pass, when you are come to the land which the Lord will give you, that you shall make a service and a sacrifice, saying, 'It is the service of the Lord's passover, Who passed over the houses of the children of Israel in the land of Egypt, and harmed them not.' "

And it came to pass, when at midnight the Lord smote all the firstborn in the land of Egypt, that the Pharaoh rose up in the night. And he called for Moses, and said, "Rise up and go forth from among my people, both you and the children of Israel. Go serve the Lord."

47

The children of Israel went forth from the land of Egypt according to the word of Moses. And God led them through the wilderness by the Red Sea. He went before them by day in a pillar of cloud to lead them on the way, and by night in a pillar of fire to give them light.

Now it was told to Pharaoh that the people had fled. And the heart of Pharaoh and of his servants was turned against the people, and they said, "Why have we done this? Why have we let our servants, the people of Israel, go?"

And Pharaoh made ready his chariot, and took six hundred chosen chariots and all the chariots of Egypt, and captains over every one. And he followed after the children of Israel and overtook them where they were encamped by the sea. And when Pharaoh drew near, the children of Israel lifted up their eyes; and behold, the Egyptians marched after them.

Then the children of Israel were afraid, and cried out unto the Lord. And they said unto Moses, "Have you taken us away to die in the wilderness? Why did you lead us forth from the land of the Egyptians? Let us alone, that we may serve Pharaoh. For that is better than to die in the wilderness."

And Moses said, "Fear not, stand still and see what the Lord will show to you this day. The Lord will fight for you, and you shall hold your peace."

And the angel of God which went before the camp of Israel, now went behind; and the pillar of cloud went behind them. And it stood between the two camps. It was a cloud of darkness to the Egyptians, but it gave light by night to the children of Israel. And neither came near the other all night.

Now in the night Moses stretched out his hand over the sea, and the Lord caused the sea to go back. An east wind blew all night and made the sea dry land. And in the morning, the children of Israel went into the midst of the sea upon dry ground. And the waters were a wall on their right hand and on their left.

And the Egyptians rose and went in after
them to the midst of the sea, even all Pharaoh's
horses, his chariots, and his horsemen. And the
Lord said unto Moses, "Stretch out your hand
over the sea."

50

Moses stretched out his hand. And the waters
returned and covered the chariots, the horsemen, and all the hosts of Pharaoh, so that they
drowned. And not so much as one of them was
left alive.

Thus the Lord saved Israel that day out of the hand of the Egyptians. Israel saw the great work of the Lord; and the people feared Him and believed the Lord and His servant Moses.

Then sang Moses and the children of Israel this song unto the Lord:

> I will sing unto the Lord, for He hath triumphed
> gloriously.
> The horse and his rider hath He thrown into the sea.
> The Lord is my strength and song,
> And he is become my salvation . . . .
>
> The Lord is a man of war;
> The Lord is His name.
> Pharaoh's chariots and his hosts hath He cast
> into the sea:
> His chosen captains also are drowned in the Red Sea.
> The depths have covered them;
> They sank to the bottom as a stone.
>
> Who is like unto Thee, O Lord, among gods?
> Who is like Thee, glorious in holiness,
> Fearful in praises, doing wonders?
> Thou stretchedst out Thy right hand,
> The earth swallowed them.
> Thou in mercy hast led forth the people which Thou
> hast saved;
> Thou hast guided them in Thy strength unto Thy holy
> dwelling . . . .
>
> The Lord shall reign for ever and ever.

And Miriam the prophetess, who was the
sister of Moses, took a timbrel in her hand.
She beat upon the small drum to make music;
and all the women went out after her with
timbrels, and they danced. And Miriam answered them:

Sing ye to the Lord, for He hath triumphed gloriously;
The horse and his rider hath He thrown into the sea.

THE TABLETS
OF STONE

In the third month after the children of Israel
were gone forth out of the land of Egypt, they
came into the wilderness of Sinai. They pitched
their tents in the desert at the foot of the mountain of Sinai. And Moses went up to the mount
unto God; and the Lord called unto him out of
the mountain, saying:

"Thus shall you tell the children of Israel:
'You have seen with what punishments I visited
the Egyptians and how I bore you, as on eagles'
wings, and brought you out of the land in safety.
Now, therefore, obey My voice, keep My covenant, and you shall be a treasure unto Me above
all people; for the earth is Mine.' "

And Moses went down from the mount unto
the people to prepare them for the word of the
Lord; and they washed their clothes. And he
said to them, "Be ready on the third day."

And it came to pass on the third day, in the morning, that there were thunders and lightnings, and a thick cloud upon the mount of Sinai. And the voice of the trumpet was exceeding loud, and the people trembled. And Moses brought the people forth from their camp to meet with God, and they stood at the foot of the mount. And Mount Sinai was covered with smoke because the Lord descended upon it in fire; and the smoke rose as from a furnace and the whole mountain shook greatly. And when the voice of the trumpet sounded long and grew louder, Moses spoke and the Lord answered him. And the Lord came down upon Mount Sinai, and He called upon Moses. And Moses went up to the top of the mountain.

And God spoke to Moses, saying, "I am the Lord your God, who has brought you out of the land of Egypt, out of the house of bondage. These are My laws. And I will show mercy unto the thousands who love Me and keep My commandments:

Thou shalt have no other gods before me.

Thou shalt not bow thyself down to any graven image, or any likeness of any thing that is in the heaven above, or in the earth beneath, or in the water below the earth.

Thou shalt not take the name of the Lord thy God in vain.

Remember the Sabbath day, to keep it holy. Six days shalt thou labor, and do all thy work, but the seventh day is the Sabbath day of the Lord thy God. For in six days the Lord made heaven and earth, the sea and all that is in it; and rested the seventh day.

Honor thy father and thy mother, that thy days may be long in the land which the Lord thy God giveth thee.

Thou shalt not kill.

Thou shalt not commit adultery.

Thou shalt not steal.

Thou shalt not speak falsely against thy neighbor.

Thou shalt not covet thy neighbor's goods.

And these are the Lord's ten commandments.

When the people saw the thunder and the lightning, and the mountain smoking, and when they heard the noise of the trumpet, they were afraid and stood back.

But Moses reassured them, and said to them, "Fear not." Then he went back into the thick darkness where God was.

The Lord spoke many other laws to Moses. And when He had finished speaking, He gave unto Moses two tablets of stone upon which were the words of the law, written with the finger of God.

And when Moses came down from the mountain with the tablets of stone in his hands, his face shone, though he knew it not.

When the children of Israel saw Moses, and beheld that his face shone, they were afraid to come near him. And Moses called unto the rulers of the people, and they answered him; and Moses talked with them. And then all the children of Isarel came near; and Moses gave them the laws and commandments which the Lord had spoken to him on Mount Sinai.

THE GOLDEN CALF

Now while Moses was upon Mount Sinai, Aaron the brother of Moses became the leader of the children of Israel. The people gathered themselves together and said unto him, "Make us gods, which shall go before us. As for this Moses, the man that brought us up out of the land of Egypt, we know not what is become of him. He has not returned unto us."

And Aaron said unto them, "Break off the golden earrings which are in the ears of your wives, of your sons, of your daughters, and bring them unto me."

And all the people broke the golden earrings which were in their ears and brought them unto Aaron. And he melted them and made a golden calf, and fashioned it with a graving tool. And they said, "These be the gods, O Israel, which brought you out of the land of Egypt."

Aaron built an altar before the golden calf. And he made a proclamation, and said, "Tomorrow is a feast of the Lord."

And the people rose up early and offered burnt offerings; and they sat down to eat and drink, and rose up to play. Greatly did they rejoice.

On Mount Sinai, the voice of the Lord said to Moses, "Get you down off the mountain; for your people have turned aside out of the way I commanded them. They have made a golden calf and worshiped it. My wrath has waxed hot against them. Go you into the Promised Land whither you are journeying, a land flowing with milk and honey. But I will not go with you or with your people lest, in My anger, I utterly consume them."

Moses went down from Mount Sinai. And a man came to him, saying, "There is a noise of war in the camp."

And Moses answered, "It is not the voice of those that shout for victory nor is it the voice of those that cry because they are overcome, but the noise of singing that I hear."

And when Moses saw the calf and the dancing, his wrath was very great. He took the calf which they had made and burned it in the fire and ground it to powder and strewed it upon the water and made the children of Israel drink of it.

And Moses said, "You have sinned a great sin. The Lord has turned His face from you; He will surely destroy you. He will not be with you in the Promised Land, but will blot you out of His book so that not one of you remains."

The people mourned, for they feared the Lord would consume them, even unto the women and children.

When Moses heard their cries, he took the tabernacle of the Lord and pitched it far from the camp. And those that sought the Lord followed Moses. They rose up, and every man stood at his tent door and looked after him.

And it came to pass, as Moses entered into the tabernacle, that the cloudy pillar descended and stood at the door; and the Lord talked to Moses, face to face, as a man speaks unto his friend.

And Moses said unto the Lord, "Now, therefore, I pray You declare the way that I may find grace in Your sight; and consider that this nation is Your people. And I beseech You, show me Your glory."

And the Lord said, "My presence shall go with you, and I will give you rest. I will make all My goodness pass before you, and proclaim the name of the Lord before you."

Then Moses turned again to the children of Israel. When they saw him, they knew the Lord was with them and with Moses, who had brought them forth out of the land of Egypt.

DAVID AND GOLIATH

It came to pass that when the children of Israel reached the land promised to them by the Lord, and conquered the peoples in it, the land was divided by lot among the nine tribes of Israel. A certain piece of land was given to the children of Judah, Joseph's brother. They settled on the land, and prospered, and after many years the land itself came to be called Judah.

In the days when Saul was King of Israel, there lived near the city of Bethlehem in Judah, Jesse, a godly man, and his eight sons. He was grown old and burdened with years. His three oldest sons, Eliab, Abinadab, and Shammah, had followed Saul into battle. But the youngest son, David, kept his father's sheep.

Now the Philistines, who were enemies of the Hebrews, were camped on one side of the mountains, seeking to destroy Israel. On the other side, with the valley between them, were the armed hosts of Israel. And the two armies prepared for battle.

Now there went out from the camp of the Philistines a champion, Goliath of Gath. He was tall as a man and half as tall again. He wore on his head a helmet of brass; he was clothed with heavy armor; greaves of brass were on his legs, and a shield of brass between his shoulders. The staff of his spear was heavy, and his spear's head weighed six hundred shekels of iron.

When Goliath stood in the sun, he was like a tower of brass, and the brightness of his armor struck the hearts of the men of Israel with fear.

His voice was like a trumpet of brass as he called out across the valley of peril:

"Choose you a man for your people. Let him come down to me. If he is able to fight with me and kill me then we, the Philistines, will be your servants. But if I prevail against him, then you shall be our servants, you and your children all the years of your life."

For forty days, morning and evening, Goliath strode between the two armies. But no one in all Israel stepped forth to do battle with him.

Now it came to pass that at evening, when his sheep were safe in the fold, David went to the house of Jesse his father. And Jesse spoke to him, saying:

"Take a measure of this parched corn and these ten loaves, and carry them to your brothers. Take also these ten cheeses to the captain of the men with whom your brothers are encamped. Look, and see well how it fares with your brothers."

David rose early in the morning and left the sheep with a keeper. When he came to the vale of Elah, where the men of Israel were, he left all that he had brought with the keeper of the King's goods. And he hastened forward into the valley, where Saul's army was already in battle.

And David saw Goliath the champion, and heard his voice echoing among the hills:

"Send you a man who will dare to come down and do battle with me."

The men of Israel fled before Goliath, and were sore afraid. And they said to David:

"Have you not seen this giant Goliath? Have you not heard his words?"

And David answered them: "Yea, forty days, morning and evening, have I heard him." And he asked, "What will be the reward of the man who kills this Philistine? Who is this Goliath of Gath that he defies the armies of the living God?"

The people answered, "The King will give him who slays the giant great riches; and the King will give him his daughter, and will make his father's house free in Israel."

Of many David asked the question, and always they answered the same. But Eliab, his eldest brother, heard how David spoke to the men, and was angry.

"Why have you, a stripling, come down among the men of battle, and why do you walk among the tents of them that fight?"

"Did I not bring food, and was not the reason of my coming good?" answered David.

"With whom did you leave the sheep? In the wilderness did you leave them?"

David spoke again, "A guard I set over them in my father's pasture. What then have I done wrong?"

Eliab shouted in his wrath: "I know your pride and the wickedness of your heart. You have come to see the battle."

David turned away from Eliab, and again asked of all he met, "What shall be the gift to him who takes this curse from Israel?"

66

Now those that heard David speak brought word of him to Saul the King. Saul knew David and sent for him, and he looked with joy on the young shepherd. For the lad was like a prince, though he stood before the leader of Israel clad only in his simple herdsman's tunic, a leather belt at his waist, from which hung a bag for his sling and stones. On his feet were leather sandals.

And David said to the King:

"Let no man's heart know fear because of this Goliath come out of Gath, for I thy servant will go and fight with him."

Saul answered David. "You cannot go against this Philistine to fight him. You are but a youth, and he a man of war."

And David said, "I thy servant keep my father's sheep; and when a lion and a bear came and took a lamb out of the flock, I went out after them. I smote them and took the lamb out of their mouths. I caught them by the head and slew them. I slew both the lion and the bear, so will I smite this Philistine who stands against the armies of Israel."

Saul then answered, "A mighty man and a man of strength is this Goliath." And David said, "The Lord delivered me out of the paw of the lion and out of the paw of the bear; He will deliver me from the hand of the Philistine."

Saul gave to David his blessing, saying, "Go, and the Lord shall be with you."

And Saul put on David his own helmet of brass and his armor and gave to David his sword. But David said to Saul, "I cannot go forth with these, for I have not worn nor tried them."

And David put them from him, and took his staff in his hand. He knelt by the brook and chose five smooth stones, and put them in his shepherd's bag. His sling was in his hand. And David drew near the Philistine.

When the giant saw David he despised him. For he was but a youth, ruddy, and with a fair, open countenance. And Goliath called to David in a voice of wrath.

"Am I then a dog that you come against me
with but a staff in your hand?"

The Philistine raised his sword. It was as
tall as David. "Come to me," cried the giant,
"and I will give your bones to the birds of the
air and the beasts of the field."

Then David said to the Philistine, "You
stand before me with a sword, a spear, and
a javelin. But I come to you in the name of the
Lord of hosts, God of the armies of Israel. The
battle is the Lord's."

David moved close and spoke again.

"This day the Lord will deliver you into my
hand. I will smite you, and your head from
you. I will give the bones of the host of the
Philistine to the wild beasts of the earth and
the birds of the air. The earth will know there
is a God in Israel."

The Philistine went down toward David,
and David ran toward the army of the enemy
to meet him.

David took a stone from his bag and sent it straight from his sling. The stone struck Goliath in the forehead, and the giant fell upon his face, dead. Then David ran and stood over the Philistine and took his sword and cut off his head with its broad blade.

When the Philistines saw that their champion was dead, they fled; and the men of Israel rose and drove them far from the land.

David took the head of Goliath to Jerusalem, the King's city, and gave it to the King. And as he passed along the way, women came from all the cities of Israel, singing and dancing. With timbrels they sang joyfully:

*Saul has slain his thousands
and David his ten thousands.*

Of all that saw David, none looked upon him with more favor than did Michal, Saul's daughter. And when David saw how fair she was in her raiment of fine linen, with jewels upon her neck and gold upon her arms, his heart was filled with joy. And Saul gave Michal to David for his wife.

And from that day forth, Michal greatly loved the young shepherd come out of Bethlehem of Judah. And Saul the King knew that the Lord was with David.

THE
TWENTY-THIRD PSALM

Now Saul took David into his house and would
not let him return to his father. David played
the harp in the presence of King Saul and sang
songs, which are called Psalms. And this is one
of David's psalms:

The Lord is my shepherd; I shall not want.
He maketh me to lie down in green pastures;
He leadeth me beside the still waters.
He restoreth my soul;
He leadeth me in the paths of righteousness for
    His name's sake.
Yea, though I walk through the valley of the shadow
    of death,
I will fear no evil; for Thou art with me;
Thy rod and Thy staff they comfort me.
Thou preparest a table before me in the presence of
    mine enemies:
Thou anointest my head with oil; my cup runneth over.
Surely goodness and mercy shall follow me all the
    days of my life,
And I will dwell in the house af the Lord forever.

DANIEL IN
THE LION'S DEN

It came to pass that the kingdom of Judah fell
under the rule of the Medes, a strong, warlike
nation. And in the days when Darius the
Mede ruled in the land, he placed over it a hundred and twenty princes. Of these the first was
Daniel, a Hebrew captive from the kingdom
of Judah. Daniel was chosen above all in Israel
because an excellent spirit was in him. And
Darius thought to set him over the whole realm.

It came to pass that the rulers and governors
who were less favored than Daniel were
angered, and sought to bring him down from
his high place. But they found no fault in him.
Then said these men: "We can prove no wrong
against Daniel, except we find it in the law by
which he worships the God of Israel."

And the rulers and governors went before the King, and said thus to him:

"King Darius, live forever. All the governors and the rulers, the wise and the mighty, have gathered together to make a decree that whosoever shall pray to any god or man for thirty days, save only you, O King, that one shall be thrown into a den of lions. Now make firm this rule, O King, and sign the writing that it be not changed, according to the law of the Medes and the Persians, which alters not."

Wherefore King Darius signed the writing and the decree.

Daniel knew the writing was signed. But he went into his house; and his window being open in his chamber, he went down on his knees three times a day, and prayed and gave thanks to his God as he had before. And Daniel knew in his heart how great is the word of the Lord, and mightier than the laws of kings.

Those who had appeared before Darius came together and found Daniel praying unto his God. Then they returned to the King, and spoke before the King concerning his decree:

"Have you not signed a decree that whosoever, for thirty days, shall pray to his god or ask anything of any man save only you, O King, that one shall be cast into a den of lions?"

The King answered and said, "The thing is true, according to the law of the Medes and the Persians, which alters not."

Then answered they, and said before the King, "That Daniel, a captive of the kingdom of Judah, obeys not the King; but three times a day, prays before his God."

When the King heard these words, he was sore displeased with himself, and set his heart on Daniel to deliver him; and he labored till the going down of the sun to save him. Then the rulers and governors came to the King, and said, "Know, O King, that the law of the Medes and Persians is that no decree which the King makes may be changed."

Then the King commanded, and they brought Daniel. And the King said to Daniel:

"Your God, whom you continually serve, He will deliver and save you."

Now stone was brought and laid upon the mouth of the lions' den; and the King sealed it with his own signet, and with the signet of the lords. This he did, that all might know that the thing had been done by decree of the King and might not be changed.

Then Darius went to his palace and passed the night fasting; nor was any music played before him. His sleep went from him, and he rested not.

The King arose very early in the morning, and went in haste unto the den of lions. And when he came to the den, he cried loudly unto Daniel and said, "O Daniel, servant of the living God, is that God whom you continually serve able to save you from the lions?"

Then said Daniel unto the King, "O King, live forever. My God has sent His angel and has shut the lions' mouths, so that they have not hurt me: for no wrong was found in me before the Lord; and also before you, O King, have I done no hurt."

Then was the King exceedingly glad for him, and commanded that Daniel should be taken up out of the den. And no hurt was found upon him, because he believed in his God.

And the King commanded, and they brought those men which had accused Daniel, and cast them, and their wives and their children, into the den of lions; and the lions broke all their bones in pieces before they came to the bottom of the den.

Then King Darius wrote unto all people, nations, and languages that dwelt in all the earth:

"Peace be unto you. I make a decree: that in every dominion of my kingdom men tremble and fear before the God of Daniel: for He is the living God, and steadfast forever, and His kingdom is that which shall not be destroyed, and His dominion shall be even unto the end. He delivers and rescues, and He works signs and wonders in heaven, who has delivered Daniel from the power of the lions."

So Daniel prospered in the reign of Darius, and in the reign of Cyrus the Persian, who came after Darius.

JONAH
AND THE WHALE

About the time of Daniel, the Lord spoke to
his prophet Jonah, saying, "Arise, go to Nineveh,
that wicked city of the Babylonians, and cry
against its evil and the sins of its people, lest
they be destroyed."

Jonah heard the voice of the Lord, but fled
from him and went down to the shore of the
Mediterranean. There he found a ship going to
Tarshish, a foreign city. He paid his fare and
set forth to hide from the Lord.

But the Lord sent a mighty tempest; the skies were black as night, yet no stars shone. The waves rose higher than the ship's mast; the sound of the wind was a cry of wrath. Now the ship lay on one side, now on the other. The waves were above it like mountains, and the boat was about to be broken. Every mariner was sore afraid, and each man cried unto his God. They cast all their goods from the ship to lighten it.

Jonah was inside the ship, and he lay fast asleep. The shipmaster came to Jonah, and said: "Arise, O sleeper, and call upon your God; pray to Him that we perish not!"

Then the mariners spoke to one another: "One among us has brought this evil on the ship. Let us draw lots that we may find him."

And the lot fell upon Jonah. And they asked him, "Tell us, we pray, from what country do you come and of what people are you?"

And Jonah answered, "I am a Hebrew, and I fear the Lord Who made the sea and the dry land."

Now the men trembled. They knew Jonah had fled from the Lord, for he had told them.

They said unto him: "What shall we do unto you, so that the sea shall be calm for us?"

For the waves rose ever higher, and the ship lay on her side as if to sink beneath them, and the mast was split in two.

Jonah answered them, "Take me up, cast me forth into the sea. Then shall the waves be calm. For my sake, because I fled from the Lord, the great tempest is upon you."

The mariners rowed hard to bring the ship to land, but they could not. And they prayed to their God, saying, "Let us not perish for this man's life, O Lord. Yet lay not the death of an innocent man upon us. For, O Lord, You have done as You so willed."

Then they took Jonah up and cast him into the sea. And the sea was calm.

Now the Lord had prepared a great fish, which swallowed Jonah. And Jonah was in the fish three days and three nights. And Jonah prayed to God from the belly of the fish:

I cried by reason of mine affliction unto the Lord,
And He heard me....
All Thy billows and Thy waves passed over me.
Then I said, "I am cast out of Thy sight;
Yet I will look again toward Thy holy temple."
The waters compassed me about, even to the soul:
The depths closed me round about,
The weeds were wrapped about my head.
I went down to the bottoms of the mountains...
When my soul fainted within me I remembered
   the Lord; and my prayer came in unto Thee.
Yet hast Thou brought up my life from corruption,
   O Lord my God....
I will sacrifice unto Thee with the voice of thanks-
   giving;
I will pay that I have vowed
Salvation is of the Lord.

Then the Lord spoke unto the fish, and the fish opened his great gaping mouth and cast Jonah forth upon the dry land.

And the Lord said again to Jonah, "Arise, go unto Nineveh, and preach unto it the words I bid you."

So Jonah rose and went to Nineveh. He went through its streets, where men walked in rich garments, and beggars knelt faint with hunger, where women gleamed with jewels and others wept in rags. He went about the city and cried out as the Lord had told him:

"In forty days Nineveh shall be overthrown. Because of its sins will it perish."

The people of Nineveh believed God and His prophet, Jonah, and they proclaimed a fast and put on sackcloth, from the greatest of them unto the least. Word came unto the King of Nineveh, and he arose from his golden throne; he laid his jeweled robes aside and covered himself with sackcloth, and as a sign that he and his people repented, he sat down among the ashes. And he caused it to be proclaimed:

"Let neither men nor beast, herd nor flock, taste anything; let every man be covered with sackcloth, even with ashes. Let each one turn from his evil way and from violence. So may it be that God will see and repent and turn His wrath from us and His fierce anger."

81

And God saw their works, that they turned
from their evil way; and God repented of the
evil that He had said He would do unto them;
and he did it not.

Jonah left the walls of Nineveh and went to
the east of the city. He built himself an arbor and
sat beneath it, waiting to see what would befall
the city. Jonah watched for its towers and pal-
aces to fall into dust before the anger of the Lord.

Long he looked, yet nothing stirred save a
flock of birds going out to the grain fields.
Jonah was filled with wrath that the Lord had
not destroyed the people of Nineveh. The city
still stood, unworthy of God's favor, a place of
strangers.

And God spoke to Jonah: "Is it right that you are angry?"

And Jonah answered: "It is right. It is because of this that I fled from Your sight unto Tarshish. For I knew You to be merciful even to the strangers, they that are the people of Nineveh. I said in my heart, 'And if the Lord spare this place, why then shall I cry out against it?' Wherefore now, O Lord, take my life from me."

And the Lord prepared a gourd and made it to come up over Jonah, that it might be a shadow over his head, to deliver him from his grief. And Jonah was exceedingly glad of the gourd.

And when the morning rose the next day, God prepared a worm, and it caused the gourd to wither.

And it came to pass when the sun rose, that God sent an east wind; and the sun beat upon the head of Jonah, that he grew faint and said, "It is better for me to die than to live."

And God said to Jonah, "Art thou right to be angry for the gourd?"

And he said: "I do well to be angry, even unto death."

The Lord said, "In your heart was pity for this gourd when it withered away. Yet you did not plant it, nor water it, nor tend it as it grew. How much more shall I, the Lord, have pity on these people, who know not their right hand from their left? And should I not spare Nineveh, that great city, its men and its cattle? I, your God, will show mercy toward the strangers in a distant land. And salvation is to them in a far country, even as to Mine own people, those that dwell in Israel."

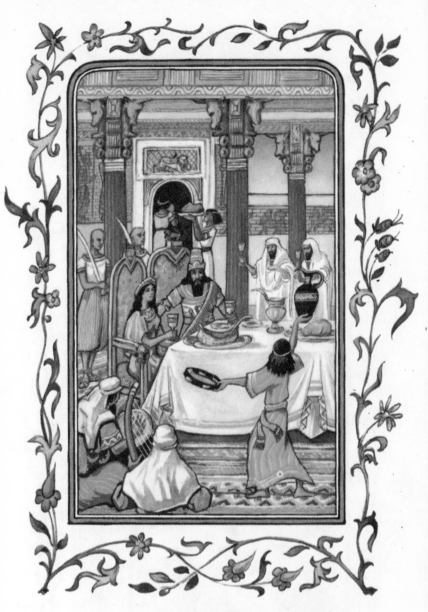

THE STORY OF ESTHER

Now it came to pass than when King Ahasuerus sat on the throne of Persia, he chose from among the maidens of many lands the beautiful maiden Esther. Mordecai the Jew had brought her up as his daughter, for she had no father or mother. Mordecai charged Esther, when she went into Shushan, the palace, that she tell not of her father or her kindred. And Esther did as Mordecai commanded.

The King loved Esther above all women. He set the royal crown upon her head and made her his Queen. Then the King made a great feast, a feast for Esther, and he rejoiced and gave gifts.

And in those days, Mordecai was a guard at the King's gate.

Now two of the King's chamberlains were
angry, and sought to lay hands upon the King
to harm him. When the thing became known to
Mordecai, he told Esther. And in Mordecai's
name, Esther gave warnings to the King. The
two chamberlains were hanged in a tree; and it
was written in the book of the chronicles for
King Ahasuerus.

After these happenings, the King did promote Haman, another chamberlain, and set him above all other princes. The King's servants that were at the King's gate bowed before Haman, but Mordecai the Jew did not bow. Then was Haman full of wrath. But he scorned to lay hands on Mordecai alone. He sought to destroy with him all the Jews in the land.

Haman sent letters sealed with the King's seal throughout the land. In them it was ordered that all Jews, both young and old, the little children and the women, be slain in one day. In every part of the land there was great mourning among the Jews, and fasting and weeping and wailing.

And Haman had a great gallows built on which to hang Mordecai.

Mordecai sent word to Esther: "Go you before the King and ask mercy for your people. Think not that you shall escape in the King's palace more than all Jews. If you hold your peace at this time, you and your father's house shall be destroyed."

Now Esther was in great fear of the King, but she bade a messenger say to Mordecai, "I and my maidens will fast. Then I will go before the King, And if I perish, I perish."

Esther put on her royal apparel and stood in the inner court of the King's house. And the King received her.

Esther said, "If I have found favor in your sight, O King, let my life be given me and the life of my people. For we are sold, I and my people, to be destroyed, to be slain, and to perish."

And the King answered, "Who is he and where is he, that plots in his heart to do so?"

And Esther answered, "The enemy is the wicked Haman." And when the King knew it was Haman who had done this thing, he had him hanged on the gallows, even on the gallows Haman had built for Mordecai the Jew.

And Mordecai was set in the place of Haman. And Mordecai sent letters in the King's name, and sealed with the King's seal, wherein it was written that the Jews henceforth should know neither harm nor fear. And in every province in every city wheresoever the King's decree came, the Jews had joy and gladness and a good day.

It was commanded that the Jews keep each year a feast in memory of the day and the month wherein they were saved by Esther the Queen. These days were called the feast of Purim, and were to be remembered and kept throughout every generation, every family, every province, and every city.

A PROPHECY

The house of Jesse, father of King David, the children of it and their generation, were like a great tree from which was to come marvelous fruit, like a shepherd's staff, suddenly blossoming. From the house of Jesse and the house of David was to come a Messiah, the anointed one, the Saviour.

In ancient days the Prophet Isaiah sang:

> And there shall come forth a rod out of the stem
>   of Jesse,
> And a Branch shall grow out of his roots.
>
> And the spirit of the Lord shall rest upon him,
> The spirit of wisdom and understanding,
> The spirit of counsel and might,
> The spirit of knowledge and of the fear of the Lord.

And Isaiah spoke:

> The people that walked in darkness
> Have seen a great light.
> They that dwell in the land of the shadow of death,
> Upon them hath the light shined.
> For unto us a child is born, and unto us a son is given;
> And His name shall be called
> Wonderful, Counsellor, the mighty God,
> The everlasting Father, the Prince of Peace,
> From henceforth, even forever.

Thus did Isaiah foretell the coming of Jesus of Nazareth. But before Jesus' time were yet many prophets, and the last of these was John, the son of Zacharias and his wife Elizabeth.

THE NEW TESTAMENT

JOHN THE BAPTIST

When the time grew near that the words of the
prophet Isaiah were to be fulfilled, a son was
born to Elizabeth and Zacharias. And he was
called John, as it was foretold by an angel of
the Lord.

And the hand of the Lord was with John.
And his father Zacharias was filled with the
spirit of God, and prophesied, saying:

> *Blessed be the Lord God of Israel;*
> *For He hath visited and redeemed His people.*
> *And thou, child, shalt be called the prophet of*
> *the Highest;*
> *For thou shalt go before the face of the Lord to*
> *prepare His ways;*
> *To give knowledge of salvation unto his people,*
> *Through the tender mercy of our God . . .*
> *To give light to them that sit in darkness*
> *and the shadow of death,*
> *To guide our feet into the way of peace.*

And the child John grew and waxed strong
in spirit. And he dwelt in the desert, and was
clothed with camels' hair and with a girdle of
skin; and he did eat locusts and wild honey.

John baptized people in the wilderness. And there went out unto him all the land of Judea, and they of Jerusalem, and were baptized by him in the river Jordan, confessing their sins. And John preached, saying:

"There shall come one mightier than I, the thongs of whose shoes I am not worthy to stoop down and unloose. I indeed have baptized you with water; but He shall baptize you with the spirit of God."

So was the voice of the prophets fulfilled:

Behold, I shall send my messenger before Thy face,
Which shall prepare Thy way before Thee.
The voice of one crying in the wilderness,
"Prepare ye the way of the Lord,
Make His paths straight."

JESUS IS BORN

In the days of Caesar Augustus, ruler of the Romans and of all lands, the time came of which the prophets spoke.

The angel Gabriel was sent from God unto the city of Nazareth, to a maiden promised in marriage to a man whose name was Joseph, of the house of David. The maiden's name was Mary. And the angel came unto her and said: "Hail thou that are highly favored, the Lord is with thee; blessed art thou among women."

And when Mary saw him, she was troubled. And the angel said: "Fear not, Mary, for you have found favor with God. Behold, you shall bear a son and shall call him Jesus. He shall be great and shall be called the Son of the Highest; and the Lord God shall give to Him the throne of His father David; and He shall reign forever; and of His kingdom there shall be no end."

And Mary said, "Behold the handmaid of the Lord, be it according to thy word."

And the angel departed, and Mary spoke:

My soul doth magnify the Lord,
And my spirit hath rejoiced in God my Savior.
For He hath regarded the low estate of His
*   hand-maiden.*
For, behold, from henceforth all generations
*   shall call me blessed.*

Now it came to pass in those days that Caesar Augustus decreed that a census should be taken of all the world.

All the people went to be counted, every one into his own city. And Joseph, with Mary his wife, also went up from the land of Galilee into Judea, unto the city of David which is called Bethlehem, to be taxed. And while they were there, Mary brought forth her first-born son and wrapped Him in swaddling clothes, and laid Him in a manger; because there was no room for them in the inn.

And there were in that same country shepherds abiding in the field, keeping watch over their flock by night. And lo, the angel of the Lord came upon them, and the glory of the Lord shone round about them; and they were sore afraid. And the angel said unto them:

"Fear not: for behold, I bring you good tidings of great joy, which shall be to all people. For unto you is born this day, in the city of David, a Saviour, which is Christ the Lord. And you shall find the babe wrapped in swaddling clothes, lying in a manger."

And suddenly there was with the angel a multitude of the heavenly host praising God, and saying: "Glory to God in the highest, and on earth peace, good will toward men."

And it came to pass, as the angels were gone away into Heaven, that the shepherds said one to another: "Let us now go unto Bethlehem, and see this thing which is come to pass, which the Lord has made known unto us."

And they came with haste and found Mary and Joseph, and the babe lying in a manger. And when they had seen it, they made it known among the people, saying what was told them concerning the child. And all that heard it wondered at those things which were told them by the shepherds. But Mary kept all these things and pondered them in her heart. And the shepherds returned, glorifying and praising God for all the things they had heard and seen, as it was told unto them.

Now Jesus was born in Bethlehem of Judea, in the days when Herod was King of that country. And behold, there came wise men from the east, saying: "Where is He that is born King of the Jews? For we have seen His star in the east, and are come to worship Him."

When Herod heard these things, he was troubled, for he feared a new leader of the people. And he gathered the chief priests and the leaders of the land together and demanded that they tell him where Christ would be born.

And they said unto him, "In Bethlehem of Judea: for thus is it written by the prophet."

Now Herod had secretely called the wise men. And he sent them to Bethlehem, and said, "Go and search for the young child; and when you have found Him, bring me word, that I may come and worship Him also."

When they had heard the King, the wise men departed; and lo, the star which they had seen in the east went before them, till it came and stood over where the young child was. When they saw the star, they rejoiced with exceeding great joy. And when they came into the house, they saw the young child with Mary His mother, and fell down and worshiped Him. And they presented unto Him gifts: gold, and frankincense, and myrrh.

Now God warned the wise men in a dream that they should not return unto Herod, lest he ask them about the child and bring harm upon Him. The wise men therefore departed into their own country by another way.

As it is written in the law of the Lord, when some days had passed, Joseph and Mary took the child Jesus to Jerusalem to present Him to God in the temple and to offer a sacrifice, a pair of turtle doves and two young pigeons.

And behold, there was a man in Jerusalem whose name was Simeon; and the man was just and devout, waiting for the hope of Israel. And the spirit of God was upon him, and the spirit of God had shown unto him that he should not see death before he had seen the Lord's Christ. And the spirit led him into the temple. And when the parents brought in the Child Jesus, then Simeon took Him up into his arms, and said:

Lord, lettest Thou Thy servant depart in peace.
According to Thy word:
For mine eyes have seen Thy salvation,
Which Thou hast prepared before the face of all
  people:
A light to lighten the Gentiles,
And the glory of Thy people Israel.

And Joseph and His mother marveled at those things which were spoken of the child, and Simeon prophesied concerning Him, and he blessed them.

FLIGHT INTO EGYPT

Now behold, the angel of the Lord appeared to Joseph in a dream, saying:

"Arise and take the young child and His mother, and flee into Egypt, and remain there until I bring you word. For Herod the King will seek the young child to destroy Him."

Joseph arose and took the young child and His mother by night, and departed into Egypt and was there until the death of Herod, that it might be fulfilled which was spoken of the Lord by the prophet, saying, "Out of Egypt have I called My Son."

But when Herod was dead, behold, an angel of the Lord appeared in a dream to Joseph in Egypt, saying: "Arise, and take the young child and His mother and go into the land of Israel; for they are dead which sought the young child's life."

And Joseph arose and took the young child and His mother, and came into the land of Israel. And he came and dwelt in a city called Nazareth, that it might be fulfilled which was spoken of the Saviour by the prophets: "He shall be called a Nazarene."

And when they had returned unto Galilee, to the city of Nazareth, the child grew and waxed strong in spirit, and the grace of God was upon Him.

THE BOY JESUS IN
THE TEMPLE

Now the parents of Jesus went to Jerusalem
every year at the Feast of the Passover. And
when He was twelve years old, they went up
to Jerusalem, after the custom of the feast. When
they had fulfilled the days, as they returned,
the child tarried behind them in Jerusalem; and
Joseph and Mary knew not of it. But they,
supposing Him to have been in the company,
went a day's journey; and they sought Him
among their kinsfolk and acquaintances. And
when they found Him not, they turned back
again to Jerusalem, seeking Him.

And it came to pass that after three days,
they found Him in the temple, sitting in the
midst of the rabbis, the teachers of the people,
both hearing them and asking questions. And
all that heard Him were astonished at His under-
standing and answers.

And when Joseph and Mary saw Him, they were amazed, and His mother said unto Him, "Son, why have You thus dealt with us? Behold, Your father and I have sought You, sorrowing."

And He said unto them, "How is it that you sought Me? Know you not that I must be about My Father's business?"

And they understood not the saying which He spoke unto them. And He went down with them and came to Nazareth, and was obedient unto them. But His mother kept all these sayings in her heart.

And Jesus the boy grew, and increased in wisdom and stature, and in favor with God and man.

JESUS AND
HIS DISCIPLES

And when Jesus was about thirty years of age,
He came from Nazareth of Galilee. And by the
river Jordan was John, son of Zacharias and of
Elizabeth. He was preaching the word of the
Lord as it is written by the prophet Isaiah:

> The voice of one crying in the wilderness,
> "Prepare ye the way of the Lord,
> Make His paths straight."
> And every valley shall be filled,
> And every mountain and hill shall be brought low;
> And the crooked shall be made straight,
> And the rough ways shall be made smooth,
> And all men shall see the salvation of God.

And Jesus was baptized by John in the river
Jordan. And there came a voice from Heaven,
saying, "Thou art My beloved Son in Whom I
am well pleased."

And the Spirit of God drove Jesus into the wilderness. And He was there in the wilderness forty days and forty nights. And the devil tempted Him. But Jesus said unto him, "Thou shalt not tempt the Lord thy God." And the devil departed from Him.

Then came Jesus into Galilee preaching the gospel, the good news, saying, "The time is fulfilled and the kingdom of God is at hand."

It came to pass, that as people pressed upon Him to hear the word of God, He stood by the lake of Gennesaret. And He saw two ships standing out by the lake, but the fishermen were gone out of them and were washing their nets. And He entered into one of the ships which belonged to the fisherman Simon, whom Jesus called Peter, and prayed that he would go out a little from the land. And He taught the people from the ship.

And when He had finished speaking, He said unto Simon Peter, "Launch out into the deep and let down your nets for a draught."

Simon Peter, answering, said unto Him, "Master, we have toiled all the night and have taken nothing. Nevertheless, at Thy word, I will let down the net."

And when they had done this, they caught such a multitude of fishes that their nets became heavy and broke. And they beckoned to their partners who were in the other ship, that they should come and help them. And they came and filled both ships so full that they began to sink.

When Simon Peter saw it, he fell down at the knees of Jesus, saying, "Depart from me; for I am a sinful man, O Lord."

For he and all that were with him were astonished at the draught of fishes which they had taken.

And so also were James and John, the sons of Zebedee who were partners with Simon Peter.

And Jesus said unto Peter, "Fear not; from henceforth you shall be fishers of men; you shall be My Apostles."

And when they had brought their ships to land, they forsook all and followed Him. So also did others, up to the number of twelve, who became His Apostles. And the multitude gathered round about Him, and He taught them.

And behold, a certain lawyer stood up, saying, "Master, what shall I do to inherit eternal life?"

Jesus replied, "How read you the law?"

And the man answered Him, and said, "'Thou shalt love the Lord thy God with all thy heart, and with all thy soul, and with all thy strength, and with all thy mind, and thy neighbor as thyself.'"

And Jesus said, "This do, and you shall live."

But the lawyer asked again, "And who is my neighbor?"

And Jesus, answering, said: "A certain man went down from Jerusalem to Jericho, and fell among thieves, who stripped him of his robes and wounded him, and departed, leaving him half dead. And by chance there came down a certain priest that way; and when he saw him, he passed by on the other side.

"And likewise, a man of the tribe of Levi, when he was at the place, came and looked on him, and passed by on the other side.

"But a certain Samaritan, as he journeyed, came where the man was, and when he saw him, he had compassion on him, and went to him, and bound up his wounds, pouring in oil and wine, and set him on his own beast, and brought him to an inn, and took care of him. And in the morning when he departed, he took out two pence, and gave them to the innkeeper, and said unto him, 'Take care of him; and whatsoever more you spend, when I come again, I will repay you.'

"Which now of these three, think you, was the neighbor unto him that fell among thieves?"

And the lawyer answered, "He that showed mercy on him."

Then said Jesus unto him, "Go, and do you likewise."

And Jesus' disciples pondered in their hearts all the words He had spoken, that they might remember them.

JESUS AND
THE MULTITUDE

Now Jesus took His disciples and went aside
privately into a desert place belonging to the
city called Bethsaida.

And the people, when they knew it, followed Him; and He received them and spoke
unto them of the kingdom of God, and healed
them that had need of healing.

And when the day began to wear away,
then came the Twelve, and they said unto Him,
"Send the multitude away, that they may go
into the towns and country round about, and
lodge and get victuals; for we are here in a
desert place."

But He said unto them, "Give them to eat."

And they said, "We have no more than five
loaves and two fishes." For there were about
five thousand people.

And He said unto His disciples, "Make them
sit down by fifties, in a company."

And they did so and made them all sit down. Then he took the five loaves and the two fishes; and looking up to Heaven, He blessed them, and broke, and gave to the disciples to set before the multitude.

And they did eat and were filled; and there was taken up fragments that were left to the amount of twelve baskets.

And the people marveled exceedingly.

Now it came to pass that Jesus went into the temple in Jerusalem early in the morning, and the multitude came unto Him and He taught them. Then also came the learned men of the city, the scribes. They brought unto Him a woman who had sinned, and they said unto Jesus:

"Moses in the law commanded us that such as this woman should be stoned, even unto death; but what do You say?"

This they said, tempting Him, that they might accuse Him of breaking the ancient law and so harm Him. But Jesus stooped down and with His finger wrote on the ground, as though He heard them not.

And when they continued asking Him, He lifted Himself up, and said unto them, "He among you who has done no wrong, he that is without sin among you, let him cast the first stone."

And when they heard it, each knew that in his heart was some of evil, even as in the heart of the woman. And they went out one by one, and they did her no hurt. And the woman was left standing before Jesus.

When Jesus lifted Himself up and saw none but the woman, He said unto her, "Woman, where are those that would stone you, even unto death? Has none accused you?"

And she said, "No man, Lord."

And Jesus said, "Neither do I accuse you. Go, and sin no more."

And Jesus went and sat by the Sea of Galilee. And many were gathered unto Him, and He went into a ship and sat; and the whole multitude stood on the shore.

And He spoke, saying:

"Behold, a sower went forth to sow. And when he sowed, some seeds fell by the wayside, and fowls came and devoured them. Some fell upon stony places, where they had not much earth; and forthwith they sprung up. And when the sun was up, they were scorched. Because they had no roots, they withered away. And some fell among thorns; and the thorns sprang up and choked them. But others fell into good ground and brought forth fruit, some a hundredfold, some sixtyfold, some thirtyfold. Who has ears, let him hear."

Then did Jesus declare the meaning of the parable.

And He spoke unto them, how those that hear yet understand not, and those that see yet are blind before the truth, are like the seed that withered away.

"But the seed that fell into good ground is the man that hears the word and understands it; which also bears fruit and brings forth good deeds, some a hundredfold, some sixty, some thirty."

THE SERMON
ON THE MOUNT

And Jesus went up into a mountain; and His disciples came to Him, and a great multitude. And He taught them, saying:

Blessed are the poor in spirit:
For theirs is the kingdom of heaven.
Blessed are they that mourn:
For they shall be comforted.
Blessed are the gentle:
For they shall inherit the earth.
Blessed are they who hunger and thirst
*   after righteousness;*
For they shall be filled.

Blessed are the merciful:
For they shall obtain mercy.
Blessed are the pure in heart:
For they shall see God.
Blessed are the peace-makers:
For they shall be called the children of God.
Blessed are they that are persecuted
    for righteousness:
For theirs is the kingdom of heaven.

And Jesus said, "Your Father knows what things you have need of before you ask Him. After this manner, therefore, pray you:

Our Father which art in heaven,
Hallowed be Thy name.
Thy kingdom come.
Thy will be done
In earth as it is in Heaven.
Give us this day our daily bread.
And forgive us our debts,
As we forgive our debtors.
And lead us not into temptation,
But deliver us from evil;
For Thine is the kingdom,
And the power, and the glory,
For ever. Amen.

"For if you forgive men their wrongs against you, your Heavenly Father will also forgive you; but if you forgive men not, neither will your Father forgive you.

"Not everyone that says unto Me, 'Lord, Lord,' shall enter into the kingdom of Heaven; but he that does the will of My Father in Heaven. Therefore, whosoever hears these sayings of Mine and makes of them good works, I will liken him unto a wise man, who built his house upon a rock. The rain descended and the floods came, and the winds blew and beat upon that house; and it fell not. And everyone that hears these sayings of Mine and makes of them no good works, shall be likened unto a foolish man which built his house upon the sand, and the rain descended and the floods came, and the winds blew and beat upon that house; and it fell; and great was the fall of it."

113

And it came to pass, that the people brought Jesus young children, that He would touch them. But His disciples rebuked the people and sent them away.

And when Jesus saw it, He was much displeased and said unto them, "Suffer the little children to come unto Me, and forbid them not; for of such is the kingdom of heaven.

"Verily I say unto you, Whosoever shall not receive the kingdom of God as a little child, shall not enter therein."

And He took the children in His arms, and put His hands upon them, and blessed them.

THE PARABLE OF
THE PRODIGAL SON

Now fear was in the hearts of the elders and the governors of the land because of the multitudes that followed Jesus. And the governors wondred and questioned, saying, "Does this man come as King of the Jews; and shall we then be put down from our high places because of Him and because of those that follow in His way?"

And they plotted against His life and thought how they could harm the Son of Man, as Jesus called Himself. Jesus knew in what peril He walked, but He went about His Father's business, and continued to teach, saying:

"A certain man had two sons; and the younger of them said to his father, 'Father, give me the portion of goods that falls to me.' And the man divided his living between his two sons. And not many days after, the younger son gathered all together, and took his journey into a far country. There he wasted all that he had, for no good thing. And when he had spent all that he had, there arose a mighty famine in that land, and he began to be in want. And he went and joined himself to a man of that country; and the man sent him into his fields to tend swine.

"And the younger son wished that like the swine he might eat husks from the grain; for no man gave food unto him.

"And when he came to himself, he said, 'How many hired servants of my father's have bread enough and to spare, and I perish with hunger! I will arise and go to my father, and will say unto him, "Father, I have sinned against Heaven and before you, and am no more worthy to be called your son. Make me as one of your hired servants."'"

"And he arose and came to his father. But when he was yet a great way off, his father saw him, and had pity, and ran and fell on his neck and kissed him. And the son said unto him, 'Father, I have sinned against Heaven and in your sight, and am no more worthy to be called your son.' But the father said to his servants, 'Bring forth the best robe and put it on him; and put a ring on his hand and shoes on his feet; and bring hither the fatted calf and kill it; and let us eat and be merry. For this, my son, was dead and is alive again; he was lost and is found.' And they began to make merry.

"Now the elder son was in the field, and as he came and drew near to the house, he heard music and dancing. And he was angry, and said to his father, 'Lo, these many years have I served you, never going against your commandments; and yet you never gave me a lamb that I might make merry with my friends; but as soon as this son was come that wasted all that he had, you killed the fatted calf.'

"And his father said unto him, 'Son, you were ever with me; and all that I have is yours. It was right that we should make merry and be glad, for this your brother was dead, and is alive again; and was lost and is found.'"

JESUS
ENTERS JERUSALEM

And it came to pass that Jesus and His disciples were going up to Jerusalem. And He spoke to the Twelve, His Apostles, and began to tell them what things should happen to Him, saying: "Behold, we go up to Jerusalem, and the Son of Man shall be delivered unto the chief priests, and unto the governors; and they shall bring about His death."

And when they came near Jerusalem at the Mount of Olives, Jesus sent forth two of His disciples, and said unto them:

"Go your way into the village which is near; and as soon as you have entered into it, you shall find a colt tied; loose him and bring him."

And they did as Jesus commanded them. They cast their garments on the colt, and Jesus sat upon them. And many spread garments in the way, and cut down branches and strewed them, crying, "Hosanna! Blessed is He that cometh in the name of the Lord! Hosanna in the highest!"

Now after two days was the Feast of the Passover; and the chief priests and the governors thought how they might take Jesus and put Him to death. And one of the Twelve Apostles, called Judas Iscariot, went unto the chief priests and said, "What will you give me, if I betray Jesus to you?" And they promised him thirty pieces of silver. And Judas said, "Whomever I shall kiss is He; hold Him fast."

On the first day of the unleavened bread, the disciples made ready the Passover. When evening came, Jesus took bread, and blessed, and broke it, and gave it to the disciples, and said: "Take, eat; this is My body." And He took the cup, and gave thanks, and gave it to them and said, "Drink ye all of it; for this is My blood of the New Testament, which is shed for many for the forgiveness of sins."

THE CRUCIFIXION

Now Jesus had gone into a place called Gethsemane to pray. And having prayed, He said to Peter and James and John, who were watching with Him, "Rise, let us be going. He who will betray Me is at hand."

And while He was speaking, Judas came with the soldiers of the city priests and elders. And he went to Jesus and kissed Him. And Jesus said unto him, "Friend, why are you here?"

Then the soldiers set hands on Jesus and took Him to the Roman ruler, Pontius Pilate, that Pilate might be His judge. Pilate questioned Him and said, "I can find no evil in this man."

But the crowd shouted, "Crucify Him! Crucify Him!" And Pilate washed his hands before the multitude, saying, "I am innocent of the blood of this just person." Yet he said that what they asked for would be done.

They scourged Him and mocked Him and crowned Him with thorns. And when they had brought Him unto a place called Golgotha, they nailed Him to a cross and crucified Him.

And Jesus said, "Father, forgive them; for they know not what they do."

After this, Jesus knew all things were come to pass, and now was the prophecy fulfilled; and He said, "It is finished."

And when the ninth hour had come, He cried with a loud voice, saying, "Father, into Thy hands I commend My spirit."

And, behold, the earth did quake, and the rocks broke. And when they that were watching Jesus saw the earthquake, they feared greatly, and they spoke, saying, "Truly, this was the Son of God!"

THE RESURRECTION

Now when it was evening there came a rich man of Arimathea named Joseph. He went to Pilate and asked for the body of Jesus. And when Joseph had taken the body, he wrapped it in a clean linen cloth, and laid it in his own new tomb which he had carved out from the rock, and he rolled a great stone to the door of the tomb, and departed.

After the Sabbath, toward the dawn of the first day of the week, Mary Magdalene, and Mary, the mother of Jesus, came to the tomb. And behold, the angel of the Lord descended from Heaven and came and rolled back the stone from the door and sat upon it. His countenance was like lightning, and his robe was white as snow; and those that watched were struck dumb with terror.

And the angel spoke, and said unto the women: "Fear not; for I know that you seek Jesus Who was crucified. He is not here; for He is risen, as He said. Come, see the place where the Lord lay. And go quickly and tell His disciples that He is risen from the dead. And behold, He goes before you into Galilee; there shall you see Him. Lo, I have told you."

And they departed from the tomb with fear and joy, and ran to bring the disciples word.

Then the Apostles went away unto Galilee into a mountain where Jesus had bidden them come. And they saw Jesus, and worshiped Him.

And it came to pass, while He blessed them, that He was parted from them, and carried up into heaven.

And they worshiped Him, and returned to Jerusalem with joy. For they had seen their Lord risen from the dead. And they remembered the words which Jesus spoke unto them, saying:

"Thus it is written in the law of Moses and in the prophets and in the psalms concerning Me. Peace be unto you! All power is given unto Me in Heaven and earth. Lo, I am with you always, even unto the end of the world. Amen."